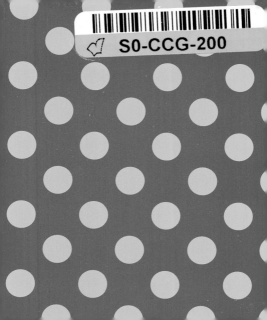

THAT'S FUNNY!

THAT'S FUNNY!

Great Lines from Favorite Comedians

Cader Books

Andrews McMeel
Publishing
Kansas City

For information write
Andrews McMeel Publishing,
an Andrews and McMeel Universal company,
4520 Main Street, Kansas City, MO 64111.
www.andrewsmcmeel.com

Design by Charles Kreloff

ISBN: 0-8362-7855-0

Library of Congress Catalog Card Number:
98-87735

Contents

Small Mysteries

Let me ask you
something—if someone's
lying, are their pants
really on fire?

JERRY SEINFELD

If truth is beauty, how come no one has their hair done in the library?

LILY TOMLIN

You will never find anybody who can give you a clear and compelling reason why we observe "Daylight Savings Time."

DAVE BARRY

Have you noticed?
Anyone going slower than
you is an idiot, and
anyone going faster than
you is a moron.

GEORGE CARLIN

Do you know how many
polyesters died to make
that shirt?

STEVE MARTIN

You ever notice when you're with someone and they taste something that tastes bad, they always want you to taste it immediately. "This is disgusting. Taste it."

ELLEN DEGENERES

If you were going to shoot a mime, would you use a silencer?

STEVEN WRIGHT

Why do dead people get to ride in such nice cars? That can piss you off if you're on the bus.

MARSHA WARFIELD

I spilled spot remover on my dog. Now he's gone.

STEVEN WRIGHT

How come there's no ethnic ghosts haunting houses? Puerto Ricans die, too. I guess even in the afterlife, housing's a bitch.

PAUL RODRIGUEZ

If crime fighters fight crime, and firefighters fight fire, what do freedom fighters fight? They never mention that part to us, do they?

GEORGE CARLIN

Dogs and Children

Dogs feel very strongly that they should always go with you in the car, in case the need should arise for them to bark violently at nothing right in your ear.

DAVE BARRY

I had a great Earth Day. I drove around with my muffler off, flicking butts out the window. Then I hit a deer. It's okay. I never hit a deer unless I intend to eat it.

DREW CAREY

Why does McDonald's have to count every burger that they sell? What is their ultimate goal? Do they want cows to surrender voluntarily?

JERRY SEINFELD

My favorite animal is steak.

FRAN LEBOWITZ

When I was growing up, we had a petting zoo and well, we had two sections. We had a petting zoo and then we had a heavy petting zoo. People who really liked the animals a lot. It was just right over there. It was just more expensive.

ELLEN DEGENERES

When I was a kid I got no respect. I worked in a pet store. People kept asking how big I'd get.

RODNEY DANGERFIELD

Having children is like having a bowling alley installed in your brain.

MARTIN MULL

Always be nice to your children because they are the ones who will choose your rest home.

PHYLLIS DILLER

If you are truly serious about preparing your child for the future, don't teach him to subtract—teach him to deduct.

FRAN LEBOWITZ

Parents are not interested in justice. They want quiet.

BILL COSBY

Experts say you should never hit your children in anger. When is a good time? When you're feeling festive?

ROSEANNE

Adults are always asking
little kids what they want
to be when they grow up—
'cause they're looking for
ideas.

PAULA POUNDSTONE

Children are usually small in stature, which makes them quite useful for getting at those hard-to-reach places.

FRAN LEBOWITZ

The way I look at it, if the kids are still alive when my husband comes home from work, then I've done my job.

ROSEANNE

I knew I was an unwanted baby when I saw that my bath toys were a toaster and a radio.

JOAN RIVERS

Never allow your child to call you by your first name. He hasn't known you long enough.

FRAN LEBOWITZ

Babies don't need vacations, but I still see them at the beach.

STEVEN WRIGHT

All too often, children are accompanied by adults.

FRAN LEBOWITZ

Domestication

I am not the boss of my house. I don't know when I lost it. I don't know if I ever had it. But I have seen the boss's job and I do not want it.

BILL COSBY

You're not a kid anymore when you can live without sex, but not without your glasses.

JEFF FOXWORTHY

Once you get married,
you always have someone
to blame. Come over to
your house and see ten
hours of slides? I'd love
to, but my wife made
plans.

PAUL REISER

Fathers are the geniuses
of the house. We're the
geniuses of the house
because only a person
intelligent as we could
fake such stupidity.

BILL COSBY

My family's house was built like the Suffer Dome. It's the House that Guilt Built. When I was growing up, I kept my front door open so that I could get cross-humiliation from my brother and sister.

RICHARD LEWIS

The latest fad, giving
birth under water, may be
less traumatic for the
baby, but it's more
traumatic for the other
people in the pool.

ELAYNE BOOSLER

When you look at Prince Charles, don't you think that someone in the Royal Family knew someone in the Royal Family?

ROBIN WILLIAMS

I got the fortunate job of playing the widowed father of three kids on *Full House*. It was wonderful, a great gig until my own three-year-old daughter, my real one, smelled my TV baby on my clothes and thought I was cheating on her.

BOB SAGET

I was raised by just my mom. See, my father died when I was eight years old. At least, that's what he told us in the letter.

DREW CAREY

They should make cards for people who you don't really care about. "You're a friend of my wife's cousin, the hell with you." "We hardly know you. What'd you expect, cash?"

PAUL REISER

I wanted to do something
nice so I bought my
mother-in-law a chair.
Now they won't let me
plug it in.

HENNY YOUNGMAN

I don't remember names, I remember faces. You should be introduced by the face, or whatever you remember about the person. Forget names. "Big Nose and Short Pants, come here a second. I want you to meet my buddy Hawaiian Shirt and a Bad Haircut."

PAUL REISER

It's weird that I have a parent who's a shrink. It's hard to think of my mom solving other people's problems, when she's the root of all mine.

CAROL LEIFER

I'm getting ready to be a parent. I just turned thirty and I'm tired of cutting the grass.

JEFF FOXWORTHY

What are the headlights on vacuum cleaners for? To turn out the lights and scare the cat?

TIM ALLEN

My mother loves to clean. She'll say, "Look at this. You could eat off my floor." You could eat off my floor, too. There're thousands of things down there.

ELAYNE BOOSLER

My parents were both cheap. I'm sure that's why they got married in the first place. They weren't in love. They just realized, "We could save a lot of money if we was together."

CHRIS ROCK

It is the solemn duty of every landlord to maintain an adequate supply of roaches. The minimum acceptable roach to tenant ratio is four thousand to one.

FRAN LEBOWITZ

Nothing in life is "fun for the whole family."

JERRY SEINFELD

You make the beds, you do the dishes, and six months later you have to start all over again.

JOAN RIVERS

Health and Welfare

I once heard about a man who never drank and never smoked. He was healthy right up to the time he killed himself.

JOHNNY CARSON

You have to stay in shape. My grandmother, she started walking five miles a day when she was sixty. She's ninety-seven today and we don't know where the hell she is.

ELLEN DEGENERES

I had my cholesterol checked and it's higher than my SATs. I can now get into any college based on my cholesterol check.

GARRY SHANDLING

I'm not into working out.
My philosophy: No pain,
no pain.

CAROL LEIFER

You know you are getting
old when people tell you
how good you look.

ALAN KING

Telling someone he looks healthy isn't a compliment—it's a second opinion.

FRAN LEBOWITZ

I asked the clothing store clerk if she had anything to make me look thinner, and she said, "How about a week in Bangladesh?"

ROSEANNE

The most remarkable thing about my mother is that for thirty years she served the family nothing but leftovers. The original meal has never been found.

CALVIN TRILLIN

You know the signs that say NO SHIRT, NO SHOES, NO SERVICE? Does this mean as long as I have on a shirt and shoes I can take off my pants and still get the bacon cheeseburger?

LEWIS GRIZZARD

Church and State

Why is it that when we talk to God we're said to be praying but when God talks to us we're schizophrenic?

LILY TOMLIN

Let's face it, God has a big ego problem. Why do we always have to worship Him?

BILL MAHER

I don't need to be born again. I got it right the first time.

DENNIS MILLER

My mother is Jewish, my father is Catholic. I was brought up Catholic, but with a Jewish mind. When I went to confession, I always brought a lawyer with me. "Bless me, Father, for I have sinned.... I think you know Mr. Cohen?"

BILL MAHER

Native Americans are angry over the historical inaccuracies of the movie *Pocahontas*. Apparently, the real Pocahontas was much younger, much shorter, and rarely sang duets with her cartoon husband.

CONAN O'BRIEN

Scientists believe that monkeys can be taught to think, lie, and even play politics within their community. If we can just teach them to cheat on their wives we can save millions on congressional salaries.

JAY LENO

Black people have it bad. At least the Chinese and Italians have their own restaurants. . . . We don't even have our own food.

CHRIS ROCK

I looked up "politics" in the dictionary and it's actually a combination of two words: "poli" which means many and "tics" which means bloodsuckers.

JAY LENO

Modern Life

The Japanese are threatening to retaliate in the ongoing trade war by making VCRs even more difficult to program.

DENNIS MILLER

The only thing that scares me more than space aliens is the idea that there aren't any space aliens. We can't be the best that creation has to offer. I pray we're not all there is. If so, we're in big trouble.

ELLEN DEGENERES

Making duplicate copies and computer printouts of things no one wanted even one of in the first place is giving America a new sense of purpose.

ANDY ROONEY

I know that experts say you're more likely to get hurt crossing the street than you are flying, but that doesn't make me feel any less frightened of flying. If anything, it makes me more afraid of crossing the street.

ELLEN DEGENERES

I don't even have a savings account because I don't know my mom's maiden name and apparently that's key to the whole thing there. I go in every few weeks and guess.

PAULA POUNDSTONE

If you surveyed a hundred typical middle-aged Americans, I bet you'd find that only two of them could tell you their blood types, but every last one of them would know the theme song from *The Beverly Hillbillies.*

DAVE BARRY

The Opposite of Sex

The cable TV sex
channels don't expand our
horizons, don't make us
better people, and don't
come in clearly enough.

BILL MAHER

Starting a relationship is like buying a cellular phone: They let you in real easy. You can get one real cheap. But one day that bill will bust your ass.

CHRIS ROCK

To attract men, I wear a perfume called "New Car Interior."

RITA RUDNER

My mom said the only reason men are alive is for lawn care and vehicle maintenance.

TIM ALLEN

There's very little advice in men's magazines, because men don't think there's a lot they don't know. Women do. Women want to learn. Men think, "I know what I'm doing, just show me somebody naked."

JERRY SEINFELD

THE OPPOSITE OF SEX

I'm at a point where I want a man in my life—but not in my house. Just come in, attach the VCR, and get out.

JOY BEHAR

My husband said he needs more space. So I locked him outside.

ROSEANNE

My girlfriend. She's not good-looking or anything. I took her to a country western bar and somebody tried to ride her. "Where's the quarter go?" They couldn't figure it out.

DREW CAREY

I want a girl with a head on her shoulders. I hate necks.

STEVE MARTIN

THE OPPOSITE OF SEX

Women need a reason to
have sex. Men just need
a place.

BILLY CRYSTAL

Women. Can't live with
them. Can't explain to the
desk clerk why you need
only one bed.

ELLEN DEGENERES

Women complain about premenstrual syndrome, but I think of it as the only time of the month that I can be myself.

ROSEANNE

Oysters are supposed to enhance your sexual performance, but they don't work for me. Maybe I put them on too soon.

GARRY SHANDLING

A secretary at a high school admitted to sleeping with four seventeen-year-old male students. As a result, she received thirty days in jail and four thank-you notes.

CONAN O'BRIEN

We had a guy in here last night who thought loading the dishwasher meant getting his wife drunk.

JEFF FOXWORTHY

I'm on my second marriage. You know you let one guy get away, you're gonna have to build a taller fence and put better food out.

BRETT BUTLER

I don't get alimony. They talk about "accustomed" to a certain lifestyle. You go to a restaurant, you're accustomed to eating. You leave, you ain't eating no more. They don't owe you a steak.

CHRIS ROCK

Instead of getting married again, I'm going to find a woman I don't like and give her a house.

LEWIS GRIZZARD

Basically my wife was immature. I'd be at home in the bath and she'd come in and sink my boats.

WOODY ALLEN

There is one thing I would break up over, and that is if she caught me with another woman. I won't stand for that.

STEVE MARTIN

Everything that used to be a sin is now a disease.

BILL MAHER

This Place

According to a new poll half of New Yorkers say they would never move out of the city. Mostly, because their probation won't allow it.

CONAN O'BRIEN

I told my mother-in-law that my house was her house, and she said, "Get the hell off my property."

JOAN RIVERS

Traffic signals in New York are just rough guidelines.

DAVID LETTERMAN

Crack is everywhere. People say it's destroying the black community. They say it's destroying the ghetto. Like the ghetto was so nice before crack?

CHRIS ROCK

People in New York are always in a hurry. When you call 911 the operator says, "This better be good."

DAVID LETTERMAN

To me the outdoors is what you must pass through in order to get from your apartment into a taxicab.

FRAN LEBOWITZ

Down south they already have cloning. It's called cousins.

ROBIN WILLIAMS

Someone sent me a postcard picture of the earth. On the back it said, "Wish you were here."

STEVEN WRIGHT

Odd Jobs

A good rule of thumb is if you've made it to thirty-five and your job still requires you to wear a name tag, you've probably made a serious vocational error.

DENNIS MILLER

The world is divided into good and bad people. The good ones sleep better . . . while the bad ones seem to enjoy the working hours much more.

WOODY ALLEN

I had a guy tell me he was a plastic surgeon, and he has two kids. That must make the "daddy's got your nose" game a little scarier.

PAULA POUNDSTONE

The Chalk Outline guy's got a good job. Not too dangerous, the criminals are long gone. I guess these are people who wanted to be sketch artists but they couldn't draw very well.

JERRY SEINFELD

The easiest job in the world has to be coroner. You perform surgery on dead people. What's the worst thing that can happen? If everything went wrong, maybe you'd get a pulse.

DENNIS MILLER

I think crime pays. The hours are good, you travel a lot.

WOODY ALLEN

Although golf was originally restricted to wealthy, overweight Protestants, today it's open to anybody who owns hideous clothing.

DAVE BARRY

If the cops arrest a mime, do they tell him he has the right to remain silent?

GEORGE CARLIN

There is a very fine line between "hobby" and "mental illness."

DAVE BARRY

If you had to identify, in one word, the reason why the human race has not achieved, and never will achieve, its full potential, that word would be: "meetings."

DAVE BARRY

Cogito, Ergo, Um...

I got an "A" in philosophy
because I proved my
professor didn't exist.

JUDY TENUTA

No matter how cynical you get, it is impossible to keep up.

LILY TOMLIN

Original thought is like original sin—both happened before you were born to people you could not possibly have met.

FRAN LEBOWITZ

Some people think of the glass as half full. Some people think of the glass as half empty. I think of the glass as too big.

GEORGE CARLIN

It's a penny for your
thoughts and you put in
your two cents worth, so
someone, somewhere is
making a penny.

STEVEN WRIGHT

A penny saved is
worthless.

DAVE BARRY

Tragedy is when I cut my finger. Comedy is when you fall into an open sewer and die.

MEL BROOKS

Polite conversation is rarely either.

FRAN LEBOWITZ

Life is full of loneliness,
misery, and suffering,
and it's all over much too
soon.

WOODY ALLEN